SMART WORK + VEDIC MATHS

CHIRAYU K

Made with ♥ on the Notion Press Platform
www.notionpress.com

Contents

Preface

The methods used in ancient India are Vedic maths, and this is my attempt to convey or tell our own math. For example, in Japan, people practise Japanese multiplication, which takes time, but they do it nonetheless. Similarly, why can't we Indians follow our own Vedic math method, where some methods such as multiplication, addition, subtraction, and square could be practised in our daily lives? The time required to answer Vedic math questions is less than 10 seconds, depending on practise. In modern method we are just remembering the method without knowing how is it processed.In this we'll integrate modern methods with Vedic methods and even creating new methods. When we understand the concepts it becomes easy for us to solve the question in any matter irrespective of left to right or right to left. Well these things are not taught in schools, just remembering the process and using formullaes doesn't make any sense it's just like copying and pasting. So this is my try in conveying you our vedic methods and using it in daily life.You Might Be thinking why is the title saying " Re-establishing the concepts of Basic Maths " because we see no one is performing or using these methods (concepts) so this is to RE ESTABLISH the hidden science of basic Maths Which Deals with basic operations like

Multiplication , addition , subtraction , Cubes , squares and their roots etc. Which is to be used in our Daily Life.

About The Author

Chirayu K student of KV IIT POWAI who studies in class 8.He challenges himself to achieve his goal and using Smart work He accomplishes. Reads about The innovators and wanted to be the one. He Has resently uploaded his innovation on GOVT website.

The Chase For Treasure .

CHAPTER ONE

Book Of Your Life

We observe that the analyst creates a report and offers improvements, and then he creates another report the next month. He then compares the two-month analysis report to see how much he has progressed. While some JUST KEEP WORKING WITHOUT ANALYSIS OR IMPROVEMENT, simply adding power and power. That Doesn't help....... We all have 24 hours but still why there is a difference between the Products. The Answer is Their working style.

Like the analyst creates a report we too should create our book of life and then compare within ourself have we made any progress. But our progress should not be compared with others as everyone is different. After examining the book of our life ask yourself are you a +Time Executive or -time Executive. The Person Who Is Managing his time correctly is known as +Time Executive and those are not able to manage thier time are called -Time Excutive So lets look what are the qualities possessed by These Executives.

In the Following Sub Chapters we would be discussing few points for Time Management. I call these points as 4 Square Or 4 * 4.

+Time Manager. (+TM)

1. Have Faith On What You are doing.

When you'll have your faith on what you are doing, you'll devote your 100 % on that endeavour. As in Bhagvad gita Chapter 18 shloka 48 it is said.

saha-jaṁ karma kaunteya

sa-doṣam api na tyajet

sarvārambhā hi doṣeṇa

dhūmenāgnir ivāvṛtāḥ

Every endeavor is covered by some fault, just as fire is covered by smoke. Therefore one should not give up the work born of his nature, O son of Kuntī, even if such work is full of fault.

2. Less Distraction

When you'll have More Concentration you'll be more Productive. And have Steady Intelligence.

tani sarvani samyamya

yukta asita mat–parah

vase hi yasyendriyani

tasya prajna pratishthita

One who restrains his senses, keeping them under full control, and fixes his consciousness upon Me, is known as a man of steady intelligence.

3. Be Active (Not lazy)

When you'll be active you can devote 100 % of yourself and can achieve your Goal.

niyataṁ kuru karma tvaṁ
karma jyāyo hy akarmaṇaḥ
śarīra-yātrāpi ca te
na prasidhyed akarmaṇaḥ

Perform your prescribed duty, for doing so is better than not working. One cannot even maintain one's physical body without work.

4. Accepting Failures.

When you'll accept your failures , then only you can move forward.

matra-sparsas tu kaunteya

sitoshna-sukha–duhkha–dah

agamapayino 'nityas

tams titikshasva bharata

O son of Kunti, the nonpermanent appearance of happiness and distress, and their disappearance in due course, are like the appearance and disappearance of winter and summer seasons. They arise from sense perception, O scion of Bharata, and one must learn to tolerate them without being disturbed.

Time Management

Is Knife dangerous or useful ? it depends who is using it. Like knife in the hand of theif is dangerous as he would kill the person but knife in the hands of the doctor could save one's life.

Similarly If time was in the proper hands, the outcome would be spectacular , but if it is in wrong hands then It's simply waste.

So we have to use the time in a right way. There are 4 steps by which we can manage our time.

1. Make To Do List.

2. Mark Dead lines

3. Priorities it.

4. Implement it

Lets look into it. What does it mean ?

1 . Make To Do List :

Write the work you need to do and calculate how much time you take to complete it and make sure while implementing it should be followed.

2. Mark DeadLines : After calculating how much time would you need mark the last date for the following work.

3. Priorities it : Mark the work as Urgent , Medium , Low.

4. Implement It : Now according to your list work out and try to Complete it.

Smart Work

Now that we have have learn't about the The Qualities of +time executive and how manage our time let's come to Smart work. It's just like smart work is the building and +time executive and time managing are the foundation of the building.

Smart work is divided into 2 Which are :

1. PLANNING. 2. IMPLEMENTATION

In the planning we'll have to do the following written in Time management. But In the imprementation we have to follow the things mentioned in +TM.

When we integrate these qualities and planning skills we actually do Smart Work.

There is one more thing noticed that when one starts implementing the work he compares among his team mate or his competitors and in that mood or in that mind set he works and sometimes in that race he forgets the quality of the work and focuses only on quality which makes a huge difference. There a beautiful story regarding self reliance or self motivation.

Once there was a business owner whose business had just started and his business was of cooking he had many people working under him and they were asked to bring water from pond and were given 2 big pots. One of the worker was Gopal he carried 2 pots one which had Crack from which the water leaks and another which was perfect. Once broken pot said to itself " I am of no use to Gopal because the water he collects in me finishes till we reach the restaurant, what's the use ? " the next day he shares this with gopal then Gopal replied " No you are very usefull even better than the perfect pot, after filling the pots when I towards the restaurant I go through the garden. The water which leaks from you (pots) falls on the rose flowers and because of that there is a row of rose there because of you.

The moral is " Every one is unique even though he might not be able to perform well at something but that's not the end.... the other part of the coin says he must be well in something ELSE......

Vedic Maths

CHAPTER TWO

Adding

So, in this method, we will add as many numbers as there are digits.
1 bar = 10 number written on side of bar = 10 + number

Let us begin with a small number. Lets us solve 9 + 8 + 7 + 5.

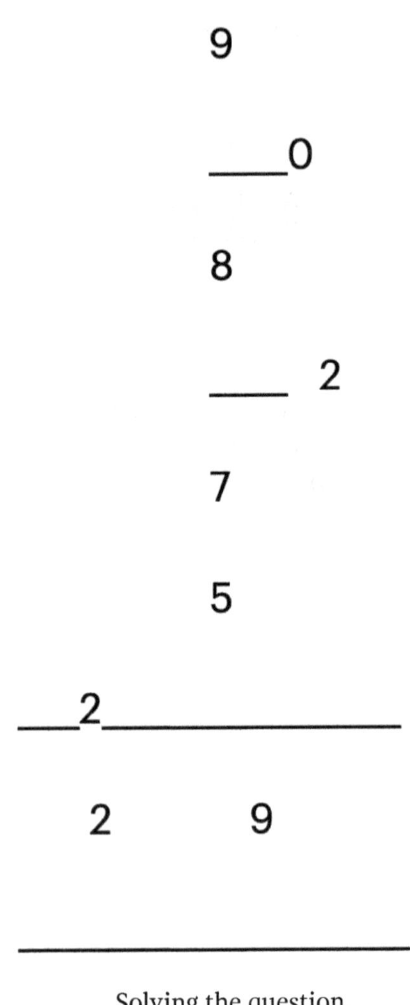

Solving the question.

Step 1: Add 5 and 7 to get 12, so draw a line above 7 and write 2 in front of it.

Step 2: If we add this 2 to 8, we will get 10, so we will draw a line above 8 and write 0 in front of it.

Step 3: Now add 0 to 9 to get 9, so we don't need to draw a bar because 9 is less than 10, so we'll write 9 in the answer box.

Step 4: Count the bars, which is 2, and then write or add 2 in the tens place. Because there is no number to add with 2, we will simply write tens place 2 in the answer box.

Like this We could use it in even in tens or hundreds digit number with the same trick. Lets see how to solve this problem : 21 + 32 + 48 + 56 :

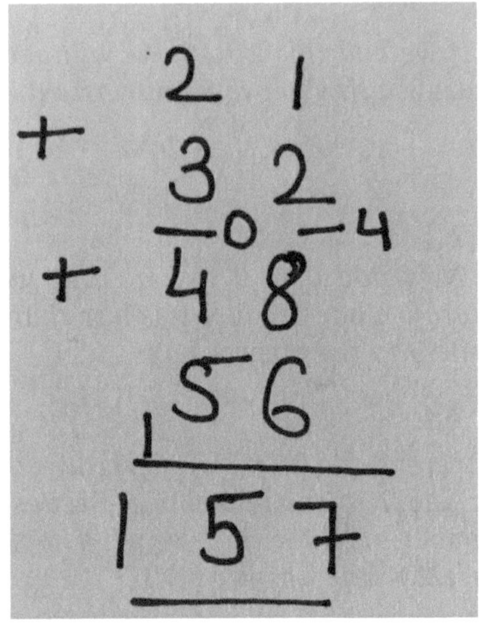

Solving !!!!

Concept

What this method is doing it is counting the tens and ones of the carry number. So , Instead of just remembering the carry we are writing the carry which makes the method or calculation even more easy, It could be used to add many numbers.

CHAPTER THREE

Subtraction

Here we will be subtracting two digit numbers, so let's take 74 - 29 = 45 as an example.
So now we will concentrate on the second number, which is 29. Evaluate the multiple of ten that comes closest to our number 29. Because the multiple is 30 is closest to 29, (74 + 1) - (29 + 1) = 75 - 30 = 45
So the answer is 45, which is extremely simple! This method does require a lot of practise because we must do it mentally.
Let's try again: 65 - 36 = 29 , (65 + 4) - (36 + 4) = 69 - 40 = 29
We can see that after getting 0 at the end, subtracting becomes simple.

Practise These Question

After Doing these questions Your concepts would be clear and would understand how to do and you will be able to do other questions like this.

79 - 48

99 -56

92 - 67

21 - 11

20 - 10

Concepts

We get a multiple of ten in the second number by adding any number, for example, 1 on both sides. So we unintentionally subtract 1-1, which gives the same value, but we get the answer and the rest the concept functions.

CHAPTER FOUR

Any Number Multiplied By 11

So, if someone asked you what 22 × 11 is, you could answer in less than 5 seconds and this technique would be very simple to perform. So, without further hesitation, let us begin our Vedic maths Technique.

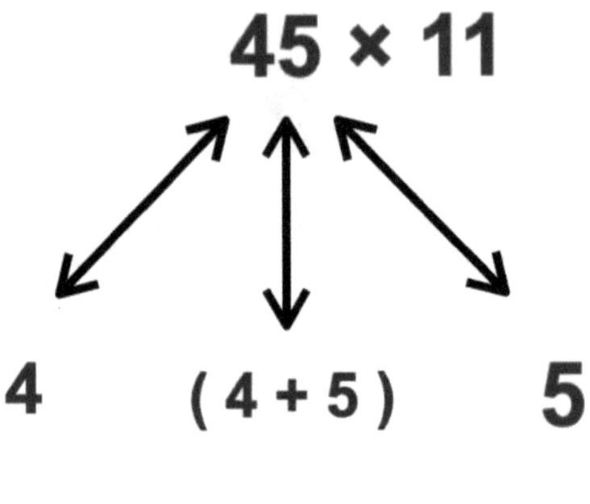

so , 45 × 11 = 4 9 5

Multiplying by 11

Using the previous example:
22 × 11
So, in this case, write the tens digit number, which is 2.
Then multiply the one's place digit by the tens place digit, which equals 2+2 = 4. Finally, write the digit for one's place, which is 2. Now arrange your thoughts, and your answer is 242. Excellent work!

Concepts

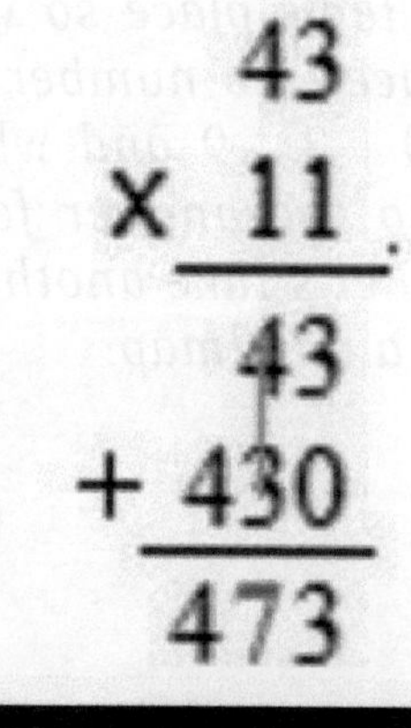

Modern Method

Here we see this 4 and 5 directly come together so we need to add these we will get 7 the same vedic method is doing as it is 11 means on the right and on the left we'll get the same number as multiplied by 1. Many questions would arise in your mind which is why we keep 0 or x before 3 in second line of our answer. The Answer is we are multiplying 11's tens digit with 43's units digit so it will be on ten's place of the answer.

Problem Arises

Now when doing 39 x 11 we'll have problem doing it using vedic maths method let's look into it. We'll get these numbers: 3 , 12 , 9 according to the method but now surely this 12 can't be in the ten's place so we'll carry 1 to the hundred place (to number 3) so it would become : (3+1) , 2 , 9 and when we solve it we'll get 429 so the answer for the question 39 x 11 = 429. Let's take another example and undertand it by a mindmap:

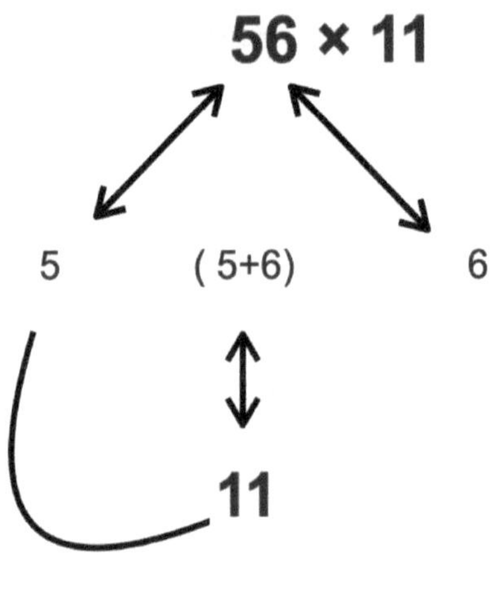

Mind Map

Nemonic

Let us assume a two digit Number as AB.

If A+B < 10 Then, AB X 11 = A, (A+B), B

IF A+B > 10 Then, AB x 11 = A + CARRY , (A+ B) , B*

** Denotes = after doing all carry process as shown in MindMap*

CHAPTER FIVE

Multiply 2 digits Number With Any 2 Digit Number

So here we will be multiplying 2 digit number irrespective of last digits

This method doesn't need any needs just the number should be 2 digit number.

Step number 1 : Draw a structure like this :

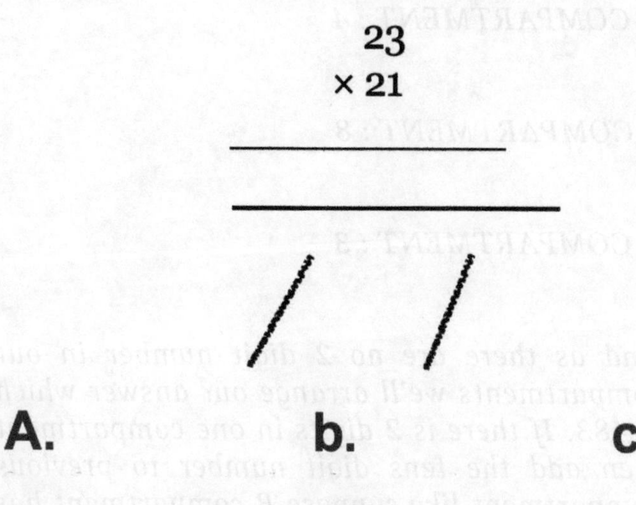

Structure

Now multiply the tens digit number of both numbers here we have 2 on the both sides. so we'll multiply it 2 x 2 which is 4 and we'll write this 4 in A. box or compartment now, we'll take the one's digit number of both the numbers here we have 3 and 1 so we'll multiply it and we'll get 3 , 3 x 1.

Now we''ll have to cross multiply and add them like
(2 x 1) + (3 x 2) = 2 + 6 = 8 , now we'll write 8 in the b compartment. Now lets see which Number is in which Compartment :

A COMPARTMENT : 4

B COMPARTMENT : 8

C COMPARTMENT : 3

And as there are no 2 digit number in our compartments we'll arrange our answer which is 483. If there is 2 digits in one compartment then add the tens digit number to previous compartment like suppose B compartment has number 12 so 1 will be added to number in compartment a and 2 will be written in B compartment.

CHAPTER SIX

Squaring An 2 Digit Number

Let us begin with Squaring any 2 digit number with a great method. So let's take an example let it be 31 square.

So for getting the answer we'll draw 3 lines. ____A______ , ______B______ , ______C_______ So on the line A we'll write the square of number's tens digit number here it is 3 and it's square is 9 so on the line A we'll write 9.

___9_____ , _____B_____ , _____C______. Now in the line B we'll multiply ones digit and tens digit with 2 and here we get 3 x 1 x 2 and the answer is 6 so it will be written on the line B.

___9_____ , _____6_____ , _____C______. And in the line C we'll write the square of the one's *digit number which is 1 only so after writting it becomes*

___9____ , ____6____ , ____1_____. And so here's are answer 31 square is 961.And to understand this Method more clearly this below given :

LINE A : ____Ones digit Square _____ ,

LINE B : ones digit x tens digit x 2 ,

LINE C : Tens Digit Square

and Now if on any line there is 2 digit number then we have to carry it to another line A lets suppose on line b number is written 12 so we'll add 1 to the number on line A and write 2 on the line B.

CHAPTER SEVEN

Find CubeRoot Of Any 5 Digit Number

In this We'll learn How to find out the cuberoot of the any 5 digit number so lets start with an example 15625 so now we have to momorise the cube table that you should be able to tell what numbers cube is what in seconds so here's the table so momorise it.

REMEMBER THIS RELATIONS

$1^3 = 1$	$6^3 = 216$
$2^3 = 8$	$7^3 = 343$
$3^3 = 27$	$8^3 = 512$
$4^3 = 64$	$9^3 = 729$
$5^3 = 125$	$10^3 = 1000$

CUBE TABLE

Now lets take a previous example : 15625 now the last digit is 5.

if Number 5 Comes then Cuberoot's last digit will be 5 (same) similarly it happens with the folowing numbers 1,4,5,6,9,0 and

For numbers having last digit as 2 the cuberoot will End with 8 For numbers having last digit as 8 the cuberoot will End with 2

For numbers having last digit as 3 the cuberoot will End with 7. For numbers having last digit as 7 the cuberoot will End with 3.

Method

Let us take 97336 as an example : Now take the the last digit of the number which is 6 and according to the rule last digit number would be 6 only so now it is clear that last digit is 6.

now we'll count 3 digits from right which is 336 and we'll remove it from number the Remaining number is 97. Now check this 97 comes between which cube number. 97 < 5 cube , 97 > 64 , 97 < 125 and so we need the smaller number and it falls between 4cube which is 64. And so our answer is 46.

Lets Take another example 10648 Last Digit Number = 2. skip 3 digits from right and the reamaining number is 10. 10 > 8 , 10 < 27 we'll take 10 > 8 and so it is 2 Cube. When we arrange the digits we get 22. so , 22 cube is 10648. and cube root of 10648 is 22 .

CHAPTER EIGHT

Square Root of Number with 3+ digits

This is a broad topic in which you would learn to compute square root faster it contains many chapter which are necessary to learn because without knowing the basics you can't improve so we have divided the steps in Chapters. To give importance to each step.

Below are the Chapters :

1. Understanding Last Digit. 2. Solving

Understanding Last Digit

See we can determine the answer's last digit by even looking at the number lets take an example what is 2√126

so square root 126 's last digit will be either 4 or 6

as 4 × 4 = 16 and 6 × 6 = 36 both have 6 in thier endings so you can remember the following table :

last Digits

1 × 1 = 1.

2 × 2 = 4 ,

3 × 3 = 9 ,

4 × 4 = 6 ,

$5 \times 5 = 5$,

$6 \times 6 = 6$,

$7 \times 7 = 9$,

$8 \times 8 = 6$,

$9 \times 9 = 1$,

$10 \times 10 = 0$

Q 1 . *What would be the ending of the this number* $2\sqrt{224}$?

Solving

Now let's take an example : 2√ 1521 or square root of 1521. now let's get the the last digit which can be 1 or 9. Then Skip two digits from right that means 21 are removed. Remaining numbers are 15. now check which square number can be equal or less than 15. 3 square is less than 15 , so ten's digit is 3. So answer could be 31 or can be 39. Now 3 should be multiplied by it's successor. that means 4. 3*4 = 12. now this 12 is less than 15 so that means we have to choose larger number that means 9. And the square root of 1521 is 39.

if instead of 12 we get number greater than 15 then we have to choose the smaller number 1.

Q 1 . 2√ 729 or the square root of 729 is ? Ans : last digit can be 3 or 7 becuase 3*3 = 9 and 7*7 = 9 (49). after skiping numbers remaining number is 7. square number which is less than 7 is 2 square which is 4. now ten's digit is 2. then, 2 will be multiplied by 3 we get 6 and 6 < 7 so we'll choose Greater number which is 7 so our answer is 2√ 729 = and 27.

CHAPTER NINE

Square Of any Number With 5 as Tens digit

See , This Method will be only applicable to the Number with 5 as tens digit Number Now lets take an example 54 Square or 54 × 54

Step 1 : We have to make place for 4 digit number. Step 2 : The square of the one's place digit should be written in C and D. ________ ________ _____1_____ ______6_____. A. B. C D Step 3 : The Square of 5 (always 25 only because we are only 5 as tens digit no). and we will add the tens digit number (here 4) in 25 which makes 29. And so our answer is 2916.

Like this we We can solve The question in seconds.

25 + unit's Digit Number Unit digit's Square

MIND MAP

Sometimes When we try to find the the square of 53 that means 53 × 53 But the problem here is that in the C and D place we only get 9 as 3 × 3 = 9 and the C place will be empty. ___2____ ___8____ _________ _____9____. A. B. C D So , in this situation we will put 0 in C 's place so our Answer is 2809

Concept

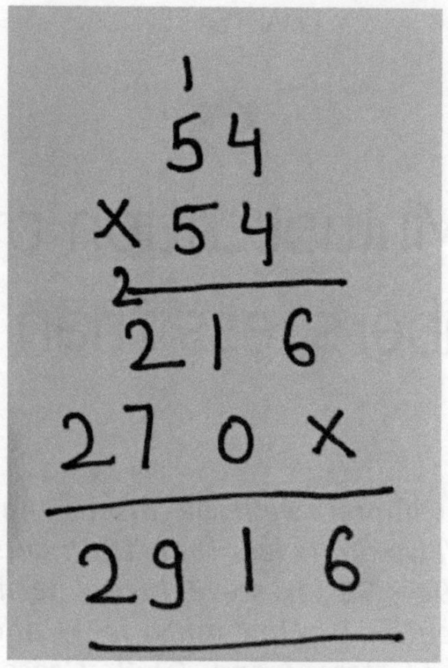

Multiplication

We see above 27 , 2 is added that makes 29 and also it was noticed : 27 + 2 = 29 = 25 + 4.

CHAPTER TEN

Multiplication of numbers less than 100

In This Chapter we'll be discussing how to multiply Two digits less than 100 . Lets take an example 94 × 95 , To solve this we need to make 2 statements : 1 . How much is 94 and 95 less than 100 ? (Here -6 and -5). 2 . Cross subtract the numbers. (94 - 5 = 95 - 6)

Now we have the numbers we need to process them so now

94 - 5 = 89 , -6 × - 5 = 30 now we'll arrange them and our Answer is 8930.

If In Statement 2 we have 3 digit Number Then

So for That We'll take another example 90 × 86. We'll write the statements :

1. 86 - 10 = 76. 2. -10 × - 14 = 140 (here we have 3 digits).

76 , (140) Now we'll have to add 140's hundred digit number to 76 's tens digit number. 7 ,(6 + 1) ,40 = 7740. So , 90 × 86 = 7740

CHAPTER ELEVEN

Was it Monday ?

Here there is an awesome trick to calculate the day by knowing the year date and month usig few formullaes .

For this one must memorise the following codes for easy understanding.

Month Code

1 4 4 0 2 5 0 3 6 1 4 6

Month Code

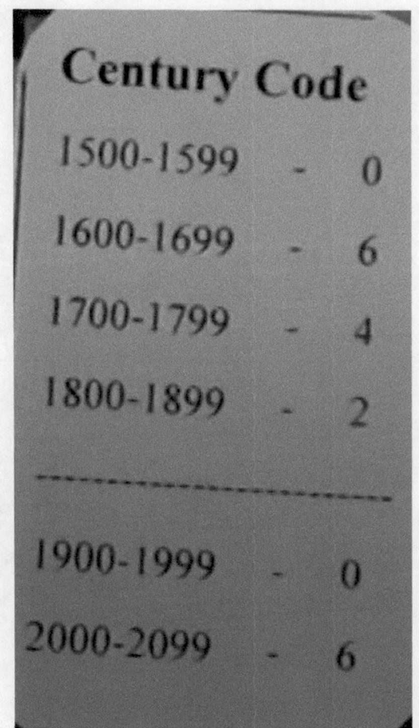

Century Code

Century		Code
1500-1599	-	0
1600-1699	-	6
1700-1799	-	4
1800-1899	-	2
1900-1999	-	0
2000-2099	-	6

Century Code

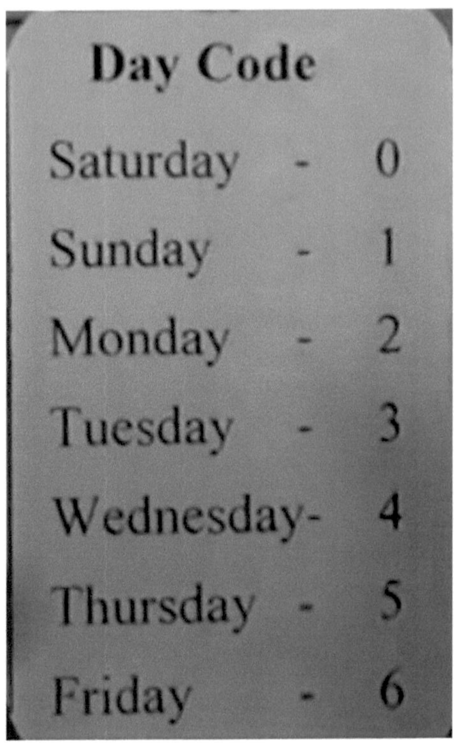

Day Code	
Saturday	0
Sunday	1
Monday	2
Tuesday	3
Wednesday	4
Thursday	5
Friday	6

Day Code

For leap year code one has to divide the year by 4 and the quotient is the code for leap year.

PROCEDURE

Now let us take an example, 15 August 1947 (Independence day)

Write Date =. 15 Write code for month = 3 Write Century code = 0 Write year = 4 Leap year code. = 11

Now Add. = 76

Now divide this 76 with 7 and check the remainder which is 6. Now according to Day code it was Friday.

Thank You

Thank you for reading this book and may you amuse your friends with such Amazing Quick mental Calculations tricks. To master these tricks you need to practise and work smartly.

असंयतात्मना योगो दुष्प्राप इति मे मतिः ।
वश्यात्मना तु यतता शक्योऽवाप्तुमुपायतः ॥ ३६ ॥

asaṁyatātmanā yogo

duṣprāpa iti me matiḥ

vaśyātmanā tu yatatā

śakyo 'vāptum upāyataḥ

Translation

For one whose mind is unbridled, self-realization is difficult work. But he whose mind is controlled and who strives by appropriate means is assured of success. That is My opinion.

9 798889 090250

Printed by Libri Plureos GmbH in Hamburg,
Germany